ONLY LOVE MATTERS

A spiritual journal inspired by A Course in
Miracles perspective

Betsy Lou Zipkin

BALBOA.
PRESS
A DIVISION OF HAY HOUSE

Balboa Press books may be ordered through booksellers or by contacting:

Balboa Press
A Division of Hay House
1 Liberty Drive
Bloomington, IN 47403
www.balboapress.com
1-(8407-4847

Because of the dynamic nature of the Internet, any Web addresses or links contained in this book may have changed since publication and may no longer be valid. The views expressed in this work are solely those of the author and do not necessarily reflect the views of the publisher, and the publisher hereby disclaims any responsibility for them.

The author of this book does not dispense medical advice or prescribe the use of any technique as a form of treatment for physical, emotional, or medical problems without the advice of a physician, either directly or indirectly. The intent of the author is only to offer information of a general nature to help you in your quest for emotional and spiritual well-being. In the event you use any of the information in this book for yourself, which is your constitutional right, the author and the publisher assume no responsibility for your actions.

Any people depicted in stock imagery provided by Thinkstock are models, and such images are being used for illustrative purposes only. Certain stock imagery © Thinkstock.

ISBN: 978-1-4525-0109-3 (sc)
ISBN: 978-1-4525-0110-9 (e)
Printed in the United States of America

Balboa Press rev. date: 11/1/2010

1

Why is it true that only love matters? Because Love is All There Is. Everything else is illusion.

A life of illusion takes many forms. Wears many disguises. God sees through them all – looks straight into our beautiful heart.

2

A heart that beats in God's Rhythm relaxes into the Love that created it.

3

We always have a choice between Truth or illusion. The Help I need to make that choice is always with me.

4

I n this new moment lies God's Grace. Something to be experienced, like the touch of an Angel.

5

W hy is it so much easier to focus on hardship rather than miracles? I only need to train my mind otherwise.

6

Grievances cloud the mind and create all suffering. Letting them go is the antidote for all pain.

7

How can unforgiveness wreak such havoc in my life? Because the natural order of things is to truly love myself and others. That is what creates harmony.

8

W ill I put my focus on Miracles or mayhem today? A choice for Miracles brings only Peace and Joy. Is there really an opposite to choose?

9

There is a deep core of goodness within all of us. It was put there by God. I want to strengthen that Pillar of Love today.

10

A competitive attitude is looking for personal glory. A cooperative Spirit is seeking a universal joining of hearts.

11

Want Divine Excellence to lead the way today. May all my talents and gifts reflect a Higher Authority's Plan for <u>Love</u> to step forward.

12

recognize my life may not feel like all sweetness and light today. But one moment of true alignment with My Source can cancel out innumerable judgmental ideas.

13

Judgments need to be brought to the Light for Divine Scrutiny. Then they will disappear and right-mindedness will be restored.

14

How quiet is the mind that releases judgments. How free – how beautiful – how filled with miraculous possibilities!

15

Do not need to prove to any others that God exists. I need only replace my own doubts and fears with an experience of Truth in this moment.

16

Beauty is everywhere today. Inside and out. I want to look around and see evidence of Totality's thoughts.

17

Fear always reflects the absence of Love. Yet, if Love is everywhere – how can fear exist at all except in my <u>erroneous</u> thoughts?

18

J udgment and anger go hand in hand. If I'm feeling angry – I can make the choice to release – rather than hold onto – any grievance.

19

G rievances cloud the mind and create a wall around the
heart. Now I need to go to my Source for relief.

20

God does not condemn or judge. I can always count on a new perception coming from Source to ease my mind.

21

Tranquility is not to be underestimated. There is no bigger gift than a genuinely quiet mind and loving heart.

22

Being open and honest with myself about what I am thinking and feeling in any moment creates an inner ease and deep sense of self-acceptance.

23

ask today to trust I am being led by Divine Guidance within. That Guidance comes from my heart, not my head. Yet, It always utilizes Divine Wisdom.

24

M y Divine Teacher and I walk the Path of Truth together today. I feel safe, protected and grounded in Grace.

25

L ove is stronger than fear, because it comes from the wellspring of Inner Joy.

26

O nly the guilty would choose pain over Joy in any moment. An innocent Spirit knows only Peace.

27

J udging thoughts and feelings of any kind serves me not. Allowing Holy Spirit to transform my lovelessness serves everyone.

28

appreciate my friendships today. They enrich my life and strengthen my heart connection to Source.

29

Today I reach out to someone who could use the Love of a friend. Now we both feel less lonely and more Divinely connected.

30

M iracles may seem far away today, but hope is just a thought away. I turn to the Divine Grace Maker in positive anticipation.

31

put spontaneous prayer first today and allow any dramas to recede into the background of my lovely life.

32

can cling to happy memories today or create a new landscape of joyful experiences. Each moment passes, offering new miraculous possibilities.

33

Why wait for happiness to happen? It is already here awaiting my acceptance. When I can let all my grievances go, I will feel how good life really is.

34

I f I am suspicious of others, then I must be distrustful of myself. This can only come from fear which is made by ego thoughts and beliefs.

35

There are so many acts of kindness to appreciate each day: a supportive friend, a smile from a stranger, the encouragement of family – to name a few. I look for evidence of caring today all around me – and it is so easy to find.

36

So much beauty to behold today. It is surrounding me and is a feeling within. I want God's beautiful thoughts to be uppermost in my mind all through the day.

37

want to relax today and remember who I am and what I came here to do. I am a lovable Child of God and I came to share that Love.

38

When I hold onto a resentment, I disallow love to be expressed. I want to be free of all grievances today.

39

There are always two ways of seeing what is happening – one way is to look through fearful eyes and thoughts – the other is to let a Higher Vision guide my sight.

40

I t is easy to respond with Love and Peace when things go smoothly in my life. The real test is to maintain my equilibrium when I feel someone has offended or hurt me.

41

" It's not so much what happens to us in the world as how we react to what happens to us in the world." (<u>A Course in Miracles</u> ©)

42

When I feel upset about something, the easy thing to do is to engage in a confrontation. A better choice is to remember I can turn to a Higher Wisdom for Divine Counsel.

43

The ego aspect of my personality does not want to resolve things peacefully. It does want to prove how right I am.

44

The issue is not to prove how right I am, but rather to genuinely show how happy I can be.

45

can only be as happy as my thinking will allow. To whom will I give the power of decision today – the ego or the Holy Spirit?

46

This is my mind, this is my life, and only I decide how this day shall be lived.

47

M ay this day be lived with passion, enthusiasm and exuberance. Sadness and suffering are not an indication of a caring spiritual life.

48

A spiritual life often reflects an inner tranquility and an attitude of genuine helpfulness. The form of that help will be guided by the Divine Teacher.

49

N o one and nothing can make this a good or bad day for me. Nothing external need influence the still voice of Peace within. It remains constantly untroubled.

50

Living in the past or worrying about the future keeps me from enjoying or appreciating the present moment. And it is in this moment that Eternal Love resides.

51

This present moment holds all infinite possibilities within it. I can use the now moment to create a more joyful future or stay stuck on a past fixated in pain.

52

create a happy future by experiencing more genuine happiness right now. My Inner Teacher shows me the way.

53

_____

_____

_____

_____

_____

_____

_____

_____

_____

_____

_____

_____

_____

_____

_____

_____

_____

_____

_____

_____

_____

_____

Blaming serves no useful purpose at all. It may feel good in the moment. Ultimately I need to take responsibility for my own happiness.

54

There is absolutely <u>nothing</u> beyond the healing power of the Divine. I am willing to relax and put all my Faith today in Miraculous Possibilities.

55

I t takes a lot of determination to go beyond appearances we do not like. Today I focus on what I want to see rather than dwelling on anything fearful.

56

A little perseverance can go a long way. When I concentrate often on my strengths, it is easier to see the wholeness in others.

57

There is a feeling of safety that comes from being at Peace with myself and others. It cannot really be explained or described.

58

The gift of Divine Forgiveness reflects God's Love for me. And this Love is endless, boundless and Eternal.

59

The ego gets easily offended. Separation and judgment are typical characteristics of the voice for fear. I choose to hear the strong and kind perspective of the voice for Love.

60

G od is grand all the time. And I can see Divine Grandeur in everyone I see or think about today.

61

What does it mean to be a beautiful Child of God? It is about limitless Love and Power being my True Identity.

62

A beautiful Child of God cares about himself or herself, the environment, the country and everything going on around the world. A caring mind trusts that God is in charge and knows everyone and everything are well taken care of.

63

Feeling well taken care of is a real gift. Appreciating that gift keeps me open to attracting more and more well-being into my world.

64

God's Grace is always present and available to me to receive. I do claim that Grace today. Now I can give to others my heart's Unconditional Love.

65

_____

_____

_____

_____

_____

_____

_____

_____

_____

_____

_____

_____

_____

_____

_____

_____

_____

_____

_____

Every moment today offers a new beginning. It often feels like I need to blame other people or circumstances for anything negative happening to me. Yet I'm in charge of how I react. May each moment truly be a reflection of God's Love.

66

do not fear anything in the world. I want that to be my attitude all through the day. I keep reminding myself – fear truly is only an absence of Love.

67

N o outside condition has the power to take away my happiness. That is God's Gift to me and it is Eternal.

68

A quiet mind easily accesses God. I can connect at any time with the Divine Silence Within if that is my intention.

69

Discord of any kind needs to be resolved. I want Harmony to be my goal today. I turn to the Peace Maker within.

70

P eace is impossible when conflict exists. I do need to ask myself, "Would I rather be right or be happy?" (A.C.I.M.©) That choice is up to me.

71

Honoring my feelings is a full-time job. I allow Holy Spirit to work with me in processing and expressing those feelings to others.

72

want to be a facilitator of joy: an uplifter rather than a nay-sayer today. I focus on what makes me happy and keeps me grounded in Truth.

73

When I am open and honest with others - I allow them to share from their heart with me. What a win-win situation for us all!

74

_____

_____

_____

_____

_____

_____

_____

_____

_____

_____

_____

_____

_____

_____

_____

_____

_____

_____

_____

_____

_____

The power of God is always within me. His Grace surrounds and sustains me. May I remember this often today.

75

There is no need to compete with anyone today. We are all free to choose between a co-operative attitude or a feeling of rivalry with others.

76

want to cherish this day. That means whomever I am with — whatever I am doing is given my full loving attention.

77

W hatever I give my attention to – expands in my mind. I notice whether constructive ideas are being given priority today.

78

"God is literally never absent from anyone in any situation." (A.C.I.M.©) I call upon His Divine Guidance whenever I feel concern of any kind today.

79

trust today that good outcomes are happening in every area of my life. When God gets involved, everyone wins and no one can lose.

80

Appearances <u>do</u> shift and change – but God's Love extends beyond time, space and this perishable world. It can always be counted on, because it is eternal.

81

S uspiciousness is a quality of the ego. And the ego always feels distrustful, anxious and 'highly' uncertain. I turn to the Divine Peace Maker to stop my doubting mind.

82

A compassionate mind is not looking to judge anyone or anything. It is at Peace within itself and looks to share that feeling of well-being.

83

rely on Love today. May all my decisions be guided by Spirit so Infinite Wisdom can prevail.

84

Remember that the direction of my life moves in the direction of my thoughts. A loving mind can only produce a loving life.

85

There is so very much to appreciate today. The laughter of children, the love of friends and family, rewarding work and all the beauty within and around me.

86

M usic can take me out of the doldrums today. Anything that uplifts me is worth giving my attention and time.

87

The key to everything is a forgiving attitude. As soon as I start blaming or judging anyone or anything – my happiness is threatened. I release <u>all</u> anger to Holy Spirit today.

88

Reactions are choices I am making. Instead of living like my life is a soap opera, I call upon my Source to create a romantic comedy.

89

I t is easy to feel good when I talk about loving spiritual theory. The real test is how I respond to upsetting moments or circumstances.

90

To fear anything is to distrust God. When I open to God's Love – all things are truly possible. I open to God's Love by forgiving myself and others.

91

M y judging mind does not want to forgive. It wants only to blame and accuse. Only my Divine Teacher can show me how to forgive, accept and love.

92

" **F**orgiveness is a natural reaction to distress that rests on error and thus calls for love." (A.C.I.M.©) Love is always a warranted response.

93

An angry mind knows no Peace. Yet it will always justify itself. There is no real justification for anger because it comes from judgment. And judgment needs to come only from the Holy Spirit.

94

Holy Spirit is the Miracle Maker in my life. If I want to receive a miracle, I need to be willing to release grievances. Past and present.

95

turn to Holy Spirit for Help and Strength in releasing grievances against anyone or anything. This Divine Help will always succeed. Failure is not an option in the Mind of Love.

96

Blaming or accusing another is natural to the ego. Being compassionate and kind are attributes of the Holy Spirit. Both are choices I can make today.

97

Miraculous possibilities abound today. Not just for a few – but for all of us. I relax into this realization and open my heart today.

98

How deeply can I show my love today? That is determined by how deeply connected I feel to my Source.

99

I n order to give Love, I need to first feel that Love within. May I be open to receive God's Grace all through the day.

100

God's Love never needs to be earned – only accepted. A peaceful mind is open to receive. But a chaotic one needs Love's Correction.

101

When I am in the moment, I am mindful of what is going on within and around me. If I feel discord of any kind – I can change my thoughts.

102

Today I start the day with meditation, prayer, or some other spiritual practice that grounds me in God. I continue to check in throughout the day with the Divine Creator of Love.

103

want my life today to be filled with passion and compassion. Enthusiasm and exuberance radiate from me, and a gentle kindness fills my heart.

104

am as interested in the well-being of others as I am in my own today. We all always have one thing in common: we want to feel loved and cherished by one another.

105

place this day in God's Hands. That means trusting in the Holy Spirit to make decisions that will turn out peacefully for me.

106

I believe in my right to be happy. In my entitlement to miracles. In freedom to be me. And I share those rights with everyone around the globe.

107

Feeling sad is a sign of not feeling my connection with God. It is a feeling to be experienced but not to be taken seriously. Only Love Matters.

108

The most I can do for my healing and the healing of the world is to feel better and better. A thriving state of being defies pain of any kind.

109

Being joyful is a full time job. It takes vigilance not to focus on suffering, sacrifice or blame. I want to put my total attention on my complete connection with God today.

110

When I feel connected to God, I realize the breadth and depth of my life. There is nothing my Source cannot accomplish for me – because His Strength is fueling my life.

111

want to feel totally lovable today. Why wouldn't I? Does God's Love change with the day or my mood? God places no conditions on how She feels about me. I am always judged worth loving.

112

People in my life reflect my feelings about myself. They always mirror back thoughts I carry around about my self-worth. May I remember that today.

113

What will it take today for me to create Peace within? An authentic desire to love myself is a good start. And a willingness to release my negative beliefs.

114

f I need anyone to agree with me, that is a negative belief that can be corrected. I want to remember – I really am ok, whether or not anyone gives me approval.

115

I t feels so good when people I respect – agree and approve of me. It is really the Divine Approval within that I am seeking. I already have everything I am looking for.

116

I remember today how constant God's Love is. Always present and available is that Love. I call upon it often and in deep appreciation.

117

My life can continue to get better and better. When I allow my mind to be quiet, my thoughts and feelings to flow easily, amazing things can happen. I turn to the Miracle Maker often today.

118

Creativity flows easily from a quiet mind and open heart. I align with my Source and allow a natural stream of imaginative ideas to come forth and be expressed.

119

J udgmental ideas about myself or others are of absolutely no value. Unless I allow Holy Spirit to help me release them.

120

_____
_____
_____
_____

_____
_____
_____
_____
_____
_____
_____
_____
_____
_____
_____
_____
_____
_____
_____
_____
_____
_____
_____

What does it mean to please myself? To live in accord with what feels right for me. So I can relax into God's Love.

121

Only God's Laws make sense. His Laws are about Love, Kindness, and feeling Peace. They transcend the laws of the world and produce miraculous results.

122

t is the Love of God that allows forgiveness to occur. There is no stronger force available to override my judgmental mind and bring my heart to Peace.

123

release my future to God today. I want to feel the depth of that promise and remember only His Grace can save me from the destructiveness and viciousness of the ego.

124

God is calling all of us to be Teachers of Love. All that is required is a dedication to Peace, Truth, and Total Well-Being. And a desire to forgive and release resentments.

125

There is so much beauty to be shared in our everyday interactions. A beautiful mind knows only the idea of God.

126

A mind aligned with God knows only Peace. And Peace begins with me and radiates outward. I turn to Holy Spirit for centering and relaxation and to give me Holy Guidance all through the day.

127

Whatever the problem, it is true that God is always The Answer. When we turn to the Divine Problem Solver, it becomes a win-win for everyone involved.

128

can disagree with someone and still keep them in my heart. It is Divine Counsel that shows me the way to do this.

129

Overlooking someone's mistakes can be difficult to do. Especially when we feel hurt. The only other option is to focus on an error and create more resentment.

130

Love really is the bottom line. No matter what our work – the only real job we have is to connect with our Source. May I remember that today.

131

etting go of our upsets is against all the ego's rules. The ego's biggest rival is Peace and that deep Sense of Well-Being that comes from our Source Conncection.

132

Being happy is also anathema to the ego. I need to remember today, "God's Will for me is perfect happiness." (A.C.I.M.©) May it be My Will as well.

133

Holding grievances is really a bad idea. It only creates distress, turmoil and a mind in chaos. The smarter choice is to give myself a break and accept a peaceful perspective of Spirit.

134

f I wait for others to appreciate me, it could be a very long time. But if I could show immediate gratitude to God, I would feel instantly better.

135

do not have to be affected by outside circumstances or events today. The only thing that can affect me is my own perspective of whatever may be happening.

136

I am so satisfied with <u>me</u> today. I'm already lovely enough, rich enough, and well enough. I really do appreciate my life and everyone in it. All of this comes from a deep alignment with God and a sense of Well-Being that cannot be stopped!

137

All my moods are determined by me. Sometimes it feels like a circumstance, event or person has upset me. Yet a happier mood or feeling is just a thought away.

138

really want to believe that it is my thoughts, not other people, that are my point of power. And that Power emanates from God's Love for me.

139

A still mind is a fertile field for forgiveness, for Love to enter and dwell with me. That Divine Love is what we are all looking to experience.

140

f I believe God is with me each and every moment, I could relax and trust that everything happening in my life will have a happy ending. I offer a prayer to feel God's Presence.

141

I t is always my interpretation of things that matters. My ego looks at things from a fearful perspective. Holy Spirit speaks to me of loving intentions. Which interpretation will affect me today?

142

There is always a peaceful resolution to everything. May I be willing and open to accept that Guidance throughout the day.

143

check in with myself often today to see how I am feeling. Positive and negative feelings are valuable because they reveal whether I am moving towards or away from Divine Love.

144

Feelings are a wonderful Guide to Peace. And all feelings can lead there depending on how I use them. I invite in Holy Spirit as the Divine Processor of my emotional life.

145

remember that Holy Spirit is the... "mechanism of miracles". I want Miracles today, I expect them and am open to receive this Love.

146

I say "yes" to My Life today and everything happening in it. May all things be used for everyone's Highest Good. I want to learn God's Lessons gently, easily and with gratitude.

147

help people most when I hold to their strength and well-being. It is of no real value to commiserate with others. I still am loving and caring in the most beneficial way for us all.

148

I decide today to be part of the Solution to any problem happening around me – instead of being part of the problem.

149

May I speak my Truth today as honestly as I can. Without defensiveness or attack of any kind. I am guided by the Divine Communicator within.

150

When the ego is in charge, guilty thoughts dominate my mind. Holy Spirit reminds me of my true identity as a Child of God. Now innocent ideas about myself and others will be uppermost in my mind.

151

remember the value of prayer today. Surrendering to the Divine is always the Answer to any circumstance of my life. I appreciate that all my Prayers have been answered.

152

U nforgiveness is always at the root of any discontent. I reflect on this idea often today.

153

I t is so easy to get caught up in the "who's right or wrong?" game with people. Convincing someone I am right does not mean I will feel happy inside.

154

want to feel happiness and peace above all else. Because that truly is seeking the kingdom of heaven within.

155

An unforgiving mind knows no Peace. It is restless, conflicted, and needs the Light. An unforgiving mind is in big need of relief. I turn to the Divine Problem Solver within for Immediate Help.

156

There is no problem without a solution. I remember today, "a feeling of separation from God is the only lack I ever really need correct". (A.C.I.M©)

157

Today is a new beginning. It can be filled with big moments of joy or little moments of anguish. A path of joy leaves a trail of loving thoughts.

158

Every thought I hold today is molded by me. This day feels like it is made of clay – to be shaped and crafted into a Divine work of art.

159

My life is an art form of the highest quality. I express myself and all thoughts and feelings, guided by the Wisdom of My Divine Communicator.

160

S haring gossip and being critical is the opposite of Divine Communication. It speaks to the disruption of communication and wants not Love.

161

S taying centered in God is the most natural thing in the world. Everything else has no real meaning.

162

To relax is to give up resistances. To relax is to rest in God. To relax is to appreciate the beauty and magnificence of this day.

163

The Mother-Child relationship is so sacred. In fact all relationships are holy if we would see them through Divine Eyes.

164

There is an Inner Presence within that is Pure Stillness and Grace. I can access that Stillness and Grace when my heart opens to God's Love.

165

So many precious moments to be grateful for today. I intend to acknowledge them all. When someone lends a helping hand or gives a genuine smile to me, I take notice and feel blessed.

166

Repeating God's Name is one way of centering my mind. Everything falls into harmony when my mind gets quiet. I do not underestimate the Power of a mind at Peace.

167

This is a day meant for joy. To judge or feel judged is the opposite of joy. I tell myself often today: A peaceful or painful day is totally up to me. Which will I choose?

168

remind myself today – What is not Love is always fear.
I want to see everything we all do as either an act of
love or a cry for help.

169

A cry for help needs to be answered with a loving response. I ask my Divine Teacher for the most loving way to express how I feel today.

170

Feeling better myself is the biggest gift I can give anyone today. I cannot give Peace to anyone unless I feel it first myself.

171

I t is true that "healing is inner peace". Conflict does need resolution. I quiet the ego today and allow Divine Truth to solve any disturbance.

172

What I think and feel does not depend on anyone else's mood. I determine my perspective on <u>everything</u> happening in my life.

173

want to come from the most genuinely giving place I possibly can today. That giving comes from the most nurtured part of me. May I remember to take very good care of myself every day.

174

_____

_____

_____

_____

_____

_____

_____

_____

_____

_____

_____

_____

_____

_____

_____

_____

_____

_____

_____

_____

_____

_____

_____

want to keep reminding myself that everything I see happening around me can be interpreted in a myriad of ways. If I feel uneasy, I ask myself, "What is God seeing here that I am not seeing right now?" (A.C.I.M©)

175

God truly is Love. And only sees Love. Divine Vision focuses only on Happiness. Where is my focus right now?

176

My friendships bring joy to my heart. I remember to let others know today how much I value the connection that keeps us sharing the paths of our lives.

177

So much I want to share today. At home, at work, with friends – I remember today there is sharing from the heart and sharing from the ego. Heart-centered sharing is a way for me to be candid yet caring with others.

178

The best way to deal with people that are 'difficult' is to step back and let the Divine Communicator step forward.

179

become stronger in my own power as I allow Divine Power to work through me. My Source and I are connected in the Divine Energy of Love.

180

There are so many ways of healing in the world. I remember today, all healing truly does start in my mind.

181

L ove can always be counted on. Even if appearances seem to show otherwise, there is a Divine Love that goes beyond form and is always present.

182

When I forgive, I create a new positive energy around me. Which carries over to others. <u>And</u> only attracts more good!

183

Forgiving, releasing resentments, letting go of grievances all do the same thing. They all free my mind from restrictions of any kind and open my heart to Peace.

184

A heart that beats in Peace knows only harmony. And beauty. With abundance manifesting all around.

185

To have abundance, I must be in a <u>giving</u> state of mind. Today I am willing to give Love often as directed by the Holy Spirit within.

186

want Divine Love to be in my Mindful Awareness today. That Love is my very Essence, my Soul and my very Being. It is my immovable Rock of Security.

187

We all look outside of ourselves to feel secure. Yet, it never works to bring us real happiness. Abiding joy can only reside within us.

188

Why do we keep looking outside ourselves, when it is such a futile search? It is the voice of fear that keeps prodding us to go on another futile journey.

189

Right here, right now, is all I will ever need to feel totally complete and whole. May I still my mind and feel the Truth of this idea.

190

How broad are my horizons today? How much joy can I accept into my heart? I want my creativity to be boundless. Sounds like a job for the Maker of all Divine Good.

191

Refuse to play victim today. That means I will see everything happening in my life emanating from me. I can easily correct any lovelessness. Or lack of kindness.

192

A sense of humor can go a long way today. Why not laugh and smile more often? If everything is going according to Divine Plan – what is there to worry about?

193

God does not change, ever. In His Love for me. I want to believe in his unconditional Love today. Believe in it, feel it, and deeply live it.

194

The idea of a punishing God is ludicrous. That would mean that Eternal Love could change and turn into something It is not. God is constant in His Love for me. Can I say the same?

195

Only the ego is conditional and capable of being suspicious or vicious. It is the ego's distrust that makes all 'evil' possible.

196

A trust in God is my natural state of mind. Today I pray to trust in God's Love for me and to feel His Infinite Patience.

197

I intend today to have a quiet mind. Feeling the constancy of God's Love for me. The only interference could be my judgmental thoughts. I release them all to Holy Spirit for correction.

198

Holy Spirit is the Divine Corrector of all my false thinking. False thoughts and lovelessness are synonymous. They go together like a hand in a glove. Why would I want misperceptions to rule my mind?

199

To be eager and enthusiastic is a blessing. It speaks of a happiness within and an appreciation of a life being happily lived.

200

do want to be serious about God today. Which means remembering to choose joy over pain – and love over fear. What else is really worth thinking about?

201

can be helpful to others only from a peaceful, happy state of mind. A mind that genuinely wants to give to others. I cannot give what I cannot feel within.

202

Today is an opportunity to reach out. I welcome everyone into my heart and watch the wonders that come from my genuine caring.

203

There is a time for action and a time for contemplation. Reflection comes first. Whatever may need to be done happens naturally and in perfect timing.

204

Whenever something bothers me, I remember to ask the question – "What is God seeing here that I am not seeing right now?" (A.C.I.M.©) And I will be immediately answered.

205

The sooner I go to God, the quicker a Divine Solution will appear. All I need is a willingness for Harmony.

206

f I insist on being right in any dispute – even if I really am – I will only be stalling my joy. I again ask myself the question, "Would I rather be right or be happy?" (A.C.I.M©)

207

Beauty is everywhere. Even on a really drab day. Because it is an inside job first. I can always think genuinely loving thoughts. Which are beautiful.

208

look around at my life and what my thoughts have created. Do I like all I see? I can always turn to the Miracle Maker within.

209

This is a new day of infinite possibilities. I pretend I am a sculptor looking to mold the day into a work of art coming straight from the heart of Divine Grace.

210

see myself as a Messenger of God today. Looking to impart good news to everyone willing to receive. I hear the personal relevance of whatever I may share.

211

can use my body for Peace or pain today. In the service of Spirit it will reflect and give Love. Used by the ego, it will lack sacred purpose.

212

To live a calm and orderly life does not mean to live a life without Passion. I want to be enthusiastic and exuberant today, honoring the Divine Giver of <u>all</u> life.

213

Harmony and Peace do dwell within me. If I feel irritated or annoyed with someone – I will not be able to access those Divine qualities.

214

Every day I get to decide which is more valuable: a mind that tallies up the slights and hurts of another, or a perspective that appreciates the kindnesses of another.

215

The ego would keep reminding me of all the things I did right and another did wrong. That voice of self-righteousness never did make me really happy.

216

Anger always seems to be justified. Yet, it never is. It's just another excuse to judge another so I can distance myself from Love.

217

To fear Love is to fear God. Because God is Love. I need to reflect on that today in the Presence of Divine Wisdom.

218

can accept today that "the purpose of my life is to be happy". Just as I am – right here in this moment – without <u>any</u> conditions.

219

A loving mind knows that God asks no sacrifice. Ever. Of anyone. God's Mercy and Peace come to us with no strings attached.

220

When I feel deprived, I realize that my ego is in charge. Now I can make a new decision and allow Truth to direct me.

221

How beautiful and bountiful are the gifts of God. I allow blessings to be freely given and received by me today.

222

S ickness is a reminder that there is a need for Inner Peace.

223

want to make Peace with myself and others today. This can only come from the Divine Counsel within me. It is immediately available and accessible.

224

Everything I want already is within my heart. Nothing external can long satisfy me. The connectedness I long for already exists with My Source.

225

Only my wrong, loveless thinking interferes with my feeling bonded to Source. The perfect remedy for this is to turn to the Holy Spirit in deep sincerity.

226

There is a stillness within me that is eternal. I want to feel that stillness, savor it, and ultimately be it.

227

L ife can be fully and happily lived no matter what our age. Getting chronologically older can happen without deterioration of any kind. I just have to believe that it is really possible.

228

All the gentle, kind moments I have cherished about someone really are the Truth about that person. Everything else is a waste of time to think about.

229

M y ego mind would dwell on untruths. On what I might distrust about someone. Yet it is all based on fantasy, not fact.

230

There is so much good to look forward to today. So many potential delightful surprises. I am ready!

231

t all seems to come down to this: Either I am deserving and worthy of a good life or not. I want to believe in my Eternal Innocence.

232

The ego looks only for darkness and deceit. And is very set on guilt. I want to release all beliefs today that foster a fearful philosophy of living.

233

_____

_____

_____

_____

_____

_____

_____

_____

_____

_____

_____

_____

_____

_____

_____

_____

_____

_____

_____

_____

_____

_____

Holy Spirit is not limited in any way. Nothing is beyond its' scope of help. Whatever is happening in my life today can be resolved quickly and easily by such Divine Love.

234

This is a day to focus on drama or deliverance. I ask Holy Spirit to take any drama or issue in my life and deliver me to its' Divine Outcome.

235

No need to beg or plead for Help from Spirit. Just a quiet noticing of what I want, rather than what I don't want, is all I need.

236

What would my life be like without any issues or conflict? It would be so happy and filled with Peace. Actually, I can live my life today as if everything already is genuinely OK.

237

want to believe in and accept people just as they are today. Imperfections too. That makes it so much easier to put up with myself on a 'bad' day.

238

entertain the possibility of forgiving myself today for any past mistakes. It helps me to remember forgiveness truly is a "Divine Action" implemented by the Higher Self in me.

239

The Higher Self in me is not petty, judgmental, critical, or distrustful at any time. That's why it can be counted on to forgive any person or situation without exception.

240

Only the ego makes exceptions. And judges. It wants me to look for – but never find – love. Even though it is right here, right now, awaiting my welcome. I pay attention to giving Love an open door today.

241

To be hopeful is to give my life a chance. A chance to move forward instead of back. A chance to be strong, not weak. And to accept joy, not pain.

242

Feeling genuinely optimistic works. It's not a feeling that can be manufactured. It has to come from the encouragement of Divine Counsel.

243

want to see myself and others today through the eyes of Divine Vision. May I continually remember – this is a new day and we all are entitled to a fresh start without the baggage of the past.

244

I release my past baggage to the Divine Problem Solver today. I am willing to feel lighter and lighter as more and more of my unforgiving attitudes get released.

245

Every Child of God has amazing potential. We are all equal recipients of God's Grace. May I use that amazing potential to relax and be the best I may be – <u>today</u>.

246

Right her – right now – where I stand is Holy Ground. May I feel the Truth of this and keep in step with the Sacred that is all around me.

247

It's all about Faith. When I have faith in God, I believe my life will work out. I have no cares, worries, anxieties or angst to deal with. I am open to a faith-filled life today.

248

Placing the future in God's Hands is an act of surrender. It's about trusting in Love. And Miracles. And having a deep conviction in the idea: "God is fact".

249

Anything not of Love is unreal. But everything can be used in Love's service. May every action I take today be used for Peace.

250

A kind word today can go a long way. For me who wants to give it, and for the recipient of this gentle communication. I want to experience the Truth of these ideas.

251

Actions directed by Kindness are always guided by the Divine. And turn out well. But actions guided by ego have no real direction at all. And keep me in a place of futility.

252

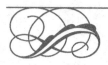

This is a bright new day. I want to be grounded in the Light of Spirit. And feel the Radiance of my Creator.

253

To extend Peace to others, I must feel it first in myself. Giving and receiving have a Divine Inter-Connection.

254

I need to acknowledge everything happening within me so I may accept all aspects of myself. When I accept myself, Love rules my mind.

255

When I appreciate the good within and around me, I create space for more good to arrive. I want to remember this today.

256

What is my Vision for today? As long as the Divine creates this Vision with me, I can trust it will contribute to everyone's highest good.

257

Today I have the right to create the most beautiful day possible. It all starts with seeing the beautiful Innocence in myself and acknowledging it in others.

258

So many colors on an artist's palette. So many colors in the art form that is my life. I allow all my moods to be seen and expressed.

259

What a gift to be generous of Spirit! To give to others freely from the heart and to genuinely care about the well-being of others.

260

Everything has a consciousness. When I look around at a rock, a tree, a bird, animal or person of any age – I respect that we are all interconnected in some way.

261

Everything responds to Love. In all my interactions today, I remember to speak from an attitude of acceptance and understanding.

262

Only the ego seeks to divide. A loving heart wants only to unite. May all conflict be reconciled today. Then tomorrow will take care of itself.

263

I t feels so good to look for the best in others. Perhaps because it reminds me to love myself.

264

God's Love is so all-encompassing. No one and nothing is excluded. There is no shortage or lack. May I feel the wholeness of His Love today.

265

God's Love shines on all of us equally. How open am I today to feel deserving to receive that Love? I pray to open my heart to the Joy that comes only from the Divine.

266

So many paths to Divine Grace. Which one feels right for me? What resonates in my mind and my heart? I commit to the path that honors my soul.

267

ask myself: "Who could use some support today? Whom may I reach out to in friendship?" Divine Counsel knows the answer and guides me lovingly forward.

268

How much time today will I spend connecting with My Source? I look for quiet moments to align with My Maker and refresh my heart.

269

How can I be too busy to find time for Peace? What could be more important or necessary for my well-being? I quiet my mind often today.

270

Breathing deeply is such a quick way to put myself at ease. I feel myself relax and release tension in just a few miraculous moments.

271

t's easy to talk about "loving our neighbor" – yet do I really feel that way? I could ask Spirit to help me release grievances and walk the walk of Peace.

272

keep in mind today that God's Laws do transcend time and space and all limits of any kind. May this belief be embedded deep in my mind and heart.

273

"I am under no laws but God's." (A.C.I.M.©) This is a good idea to contemplate deeply and often today. It can catapult me into a miraculous state of mind with infinite good possibilities.

274

Prayer, prayer and more prayer. Constant communion with the Divine is my top priority today.

275

W hat do I really know of the Divine? It is sacred territory for exploration. I offer a willingness to learn Truth.

276

No ego option has any value. Because the ego is the illusory voice of separation. Any idea emanating from fear has nothing to offer me.

277

do want to feel better and better this very day. I am entitled to Peace, Love, Happiness, and the Well-Being that comes from a forgiving mind.

278

How can forgiveness provide me with everything I really want? How can it not? A Divine Action such as this has to deliver moments of eternity.

279

All questions can be answered by Divine Intelligence. Otherwise it would not be considered Infinite Wisdom.

280

May I follow the promptings of my heart today. In every area of my life. I want to step back so I may step forward in rhythm with God.

281

There is never a reason for jealousy or competitiveness. We all have our own unique talents and ways of living our lives. May we wish each other well in all our endeavors today.

282

All outcomes are good when surrendered to Spirit. No need to try and figure everything out – but rather to relax and watch things turn out perfectly.

283

The miraculous shift inside myself from fear to love can happen today. I remember it is only grudges against myself or others that block my good.

284

So much life to live today. New people to meet and places to go. Amazing things to learn about. I thank the Divine Life Giver!

285

We are all equal in the opportunities of life. I want to view these opportunities with gratitude. What I choose to do with what has been given me is my gift to Source, myself, and others.

286

M y life is meant to be experienced, enjoyed and savored. I have everything I need to feel the joy that is already present. I am willing.

287

J oy is a word that is foreign to the ego aspect of myself. Only suffering and sacrifice are comfortably familiar to it. I want to focus on what brings Happiness and Peace today so that becomes my wellspring of comfort.

288

Everything flows to me in perfect timing. When I have a sense of harmony, ease and a positive expectancy – I then can receive all the good I want and feel I need.

289

Nothing ever is being withheld from me. It is only my worries and anxieties that slow things down. I resolve today to relax and anticipate a truly happy future.

290

want to trust today that the Universe is functioning perfectly in my behalf. Everyone else gets the same Divine Treatment _every_ day.

291

There is a Holiness within all of us that never can be touched. Not by time, nor by any external conditions. It is possible to access this Holiness since it is who I am.

292

The Greatness of Love is my Heritage. I stand proud and strong in reverence to the Magnificence that is within me.

293

God is my safety in every situation. No matter where I am, whom I am with, or what is happening. Divine Protection is always around me.

294

Today I remember to be attentive to those around me. Attentive to how I may be the most helpful and supportive. Which always means how I may be the most loving.

295

There are so many ways to show caring to others. Being affectionate to some, encouraging to others, some may want only a smile. Yet everyone can always use a touch of kindness.

296

remember today that the way I choose to look at anything is my interpretation. It all depends on whether Guidance is from ego or Holy Spirit.

297

The ego will always interpret things based on a fearful outlook. Holy Spirit will evaluate everything through the eyes of Love.

298

Fear is always a diversionary tactic. It creates an illusion of separation and makes me feel disconnected from my Source, which can never happen.

299

The words of the Holy Spirit are always reassuring and calm. They speak directly to the heart of all issues and to our individual hearts as well.

300

f I am upset in any way, I need to know there is a deeper upset underneath. I turn to Holy Spirit for clarity of what really needs healing.

301

t is always a relief to let go of animosities and to expect Peace to prevail. What I genuinely expect does happen.

302

can use the power of visualization today to picture a harmonious and happy life. It feels good to imagine the best.

303

want to give and receive only harmony today. I will be aware of any conflict that may arise and turn quickly to the Divine Peace-Maker.

304

God's Mercy extends to us all. Which means all of our sins (really just mistakes) are totally correctible with the Holy Spirit. How our errors are undone is under Divine Care.

305

Today provides another opportunity to strengthen myself in Love. I want to remember that my spiritual nourishment always comes form God.

306

The happiest of dreams always stem from forgiveness. This is at the root of all peaceful days. May I remember to forgive myself for any regrets or grievances.

307

We are all so quick to judge. And the only remedy is a willingness to let Divine Eyes give us a loving Vision Perspective.

308

I t seems like the ones closest to us often become the target of our anger. What I project out to others, I will always get back.

309

Being candid with myself is always a good starting point for being honest with others. Once again, I invite in the Divine Communicator to guide how to most peacefully share with another.

310

Sharing with others what I think they did wrong serves no useful purpose. But sharing with others what I feel they did right is a blessing to us both.

311

How can I genuinely help others today? I let Divine Wisdom guide me. There are so many ways of giving and helping others to heal. "When I am healed, I am not healed alone." (A.C.I.M.©)

312

May I start and end this day in Peace. That's easy to do when I hold hands with the Divine. And let my feet follow Paths of Righteousness.

313

Any feelings of guilt or woundedness need to be released to Spirit. Now any thoughts of victimhood can be replaced with the gift of God's Grace. Which is always present.

314

To doubt myself is to doubt the Divine. Because that is who I am at my very core. May the Certainty of God's Love dominate my mind today.

315

A gentle way works best for me. I remind myself how great a strength there is in a heart that is kind. It has the support of all God's Love behind it.

316

There is a radiance beyond all worldly appearances. This Light cannot be dimmed or extinguished. May It consume all <u>illusions</u> today and grant all of us Peace.

317

can trust in myself today, because I know it is God's Strength within me that I can really rely on. It can be counted on in <u>every</u> situation.

318

Whatever may be happening in my life – there is always something to rejoice about today. Such as being alive and having so may miracles to look forward to.

319

So much beauty in nature to behold. So many gifts to see in each season. What can I appreciate today?

320

Being happy is my right. I am entitled to Joy. Whether I accept it or not is totally up to me. I cannot receive my happiness in a state of mind that is guilty.

321

want to feel my Innocence today. That means I need to call on Holy Spirit to remind me of my true Divine Identity.

322

Justice and injustice must be opposites. One comes from Divine Mind and the other from the distrustful ego. Love is fair to everyone.

323

want to be a 'just' person today. That means tuning in to Divine Reason on all topics. Now I can step back and let God lead the way in every interaction.

324

There is always a common ground between all people. I seek for this today. I can still celebrate the diversity that can unite us from a heart space.

325

Words can be so limited. But the experience of loving words is without boundaries. Being quiet gives me an opportunity to explore the Infinity of my Soul.

326

Today is a day for clarity and peace. I turn to the Divine Director within and everything easily falls into place.

327

The ego is always looking to keep me distracted with 'non-essentials'. Its' interest is in fostering chaos. I want to slow down and put Love first today.

328

When I put Love first, I relax and am at ease. I know everything in my life is being well taken care of, including me.

329

Appearances can be deceptive. It is always what is behind the appearance that really matters. May the Love that is beyond all appearances shine through me today.

330

Focusing and dwelling on what I don't want serves no useful purpose. Putting all my attention on my good intentions does move me forward. I need to invite in Holy Spirit to join me.

331

want to remember kind moments in my interactions with others today. Dwelling on their faults is a waste of my precious time.

332

The ego looks for errors in others. And in us. Only feelings of unworthiness and guilt come from this. All mistakes are meant to be corrected gently by the Divine Inspiration that guides us.

333

P eace is on my agenda today. First and foremost. That means being willing to release all resistances: regrets, judgments, resentments and grievances all need to be surrendered.

334

What good is happening around me? What is the good news today? I listen for the laughter of children, appreciate my friends, and bless the country I am dwelling in.

335

There is so much to learn about. When I am quiet, I can tap into a Universal Wisdom that can answer all questions.

336

Guilt and sickness go together as cause and effect. Feeling my innocence and well-being also go hand in hand. I choose to breathe deeply and accept myself just as I am today.

337

When I feel hurt about anything, I realize there is always another way of seeing what is happening that will bring me Peace.

338

Everyone makes mistakes. Today I ask to see all people, interactions and events as working together for all of our highest good.

339

want to relax into God's Love today. To feel a deep sense of ease and well-being within. Unshaken by any appearances or experiences of the world.

340

God is always present. To believe this brings serenity. And hope. May I deeply feel His Presence today.

341

There is a greatness that comes from forgiveness. And a deep certainty that all is working according to God's Will.

342

Forgiveness has a power that is awesome in its' effects. It really cannot be easily described, but anyone who truly forgives is rich in Love's Rewards.

343

I know I need to forgive when I feel my heart closing to anyone. No matter how justified I feel that I am right – the only issue is: do I want Peace?

344

To live a big life – I need to stay in alignment with God. Divine energy keeps me expanding and growing in creativity.

345

God guides me in every aspect of my life. Am I hearing this guidance? I am willing to follow Divine Wisdom.

346

want to practice being in Silence today. I will be carried along by God's Grace in this process.

347

No matter how busy I am, I can always find time to access God's Peace. I want to start and end this day connecting with My Source.

348

The Spirit within us is inexhaustible. I rely on It to renew my strength and energy. Now I am ready to move forward in Love.

349

Anger always blocks my Peace. The ego thrives on feelings of upset. And welcomes a lack of Peace. I can choose to be happy instead of in pain today.

350

Power struggles serve no one. I ask for Divine Help in dealing with another that reflects my own need to be 'right'.

351

What I see in another is also going on in myself. If I feel criticized, I need to be more accepting. If I see confusion, I need to get more clarity within. When I see love, I need to share it.

352

t is always helpful to be a good listener. I give advice if I am asked, yet I want to wait and let Spirit lead the communication.

353

want to feel cherished today. That feeling always starts with my Source and can have a ripple effect with everyone I think of or meet.

354

Planning is an ego device. The ego mind is always worried about the future and looking for outer security. Divine mind takes care of our future by allowing us to surrender all concerns to It in the moment.

355

E verything is being taken care of right now. May I believe and see the Truth of this idea.

356

L ife is like a Divine Dance. There can be beauty and elegance in each step. A sense of perfect timing and an allowing of Grace in each beat of the day.

357

notice small acts of kindness today. Such as the loving patience between a Mother and child. Or an encouraging tone that gives someone hope. Even a smile between strangers stirs my heart.

358

May Divine confidence rule the day. And all doubts be easily dismissed. I hold to the certainty of who I am. And see miracles manifesting all around me.

359

Love surrounds me – embraces and enfolds my being. I am feeling so cared for. I want to sustain this emotion – forever.

360

savor Peace today. All old upsets are released. Every resentment and regret. Nothing is left but my Gratitude.

361

When I hold to the highest in someone else, I honor the greatness that abides within. This is no small gift. But it is a tribute to the Spirit in us both.

362

When I see someone else as healthy, happy, and successful, I intensify those qualities in myself. It is a win-win for us both. And a wonderful use of my time.

363

Ilusions have no place in an expansive life. They serve no purpose at all except to create chaos. But, underneath the chaos, there is always a message of Love.

364

am ready to respond to Love's Call today. Ready and more than willing. Eager to accept Peace and the deepest sense of Well-Being.

365

When I give Love a chance, difficulties dissolve. Love goes everywhere it is invited. And wants only to be helpful.

366

t is always a choice between Drama or the Divine. Just because something is familiar does not make it important. Only Love Matters at all.

367